Original title:
The Slumber Party Express

Copyright © 2024 Creative Arts Management OÜ
All rights reserved.

Author: Isabella Rosemont
ISBN HARDBACK: 978-9916-90-810-5
ISBN PAPERBACK: 978-9916-90-811-2

Firefly Flickers in the Night

In the dark, they start to glow,
Dancing softly, row by row.
Whispers of the evening air,
Sparkling lights, a fleeting prayer.

Holding dreams in tiny flight,
Guiding hearts with gentle light.
Nature's glow, a wondrous sight,
Firefly flickers in the night.

Lullabies and Late-Night Chats

Softly spoken, secrets shared,
Candle flickers, thoughts laid bare.
Whispers linger, time stands still,
In the quiet, hearts can feel.

Gentle lullabies we weave,
Under stars, we both believe.
Moments cherished, never fade,
In this bond, our dreams are made.

Cozy Companions on the Dream Train

Journeying through a velvet sea,
With cozy friends, just you and me.
Steam from dreams, a gentle rise,
As night unfolds with starlit skies.

Winding tracks of wishes made,
In our hearts, the light won't fade.
Together we'll explore the night,
Onward, onward, into the light.

Ticket to the Land of Nod

A ticket in my hand tonight,
To worlds of soft and gentle light.
Close your eyes, let dreams unfold,
In magic tales, we'll be consoled.

Whispers call from far away,
In slumber's arms, we'll softly sway.
Each moonbeam guides, a safe embrace,
In the land where dreams find grace.

Tuck-in Tales on the Wind

Soft whispers linger in the air,
Stories drift with a gentle flair.
Fables weaving through the trees,
Carried forth on the evening breeze.

In shadows deep where secrets lie,
Moonbeams dance, and stars reply.
Each tale unfolds as dreams take flight,
Tuck-in tales on this cozy night.

Silhouettes in the Nighttime Glow

Silhouettes sway in the amber light,
Dancing softly into the night.
Whispers echo with every glance,
A world unfurls in a twilight dance.

The moon paints dreams on every face,
In the stillness, we find our place.
Together we wander through shadow's embrace,
Finding warmth in the nighttime's grace.

Midnight Snacks and Laughter

Crisp potato chips, soda fizz,
Laughter spills, it's pure bliss.
Cookies crumble under eager hands,
Midnight snacks with no demands.

Stories shared between each bite,
Joy ignites the late-night light.
In the chaos, friendships bloom,
Savoring snacks in a cozy room.

A Journey to the Realm of Snores

Shut your eyes and take a ride,
To the land where dreams abide.
Mountains made of pillows rise,
Underneath the starlit skies.

Whispers guide you through the night,
Adventure waits, hold on tight.
In this world where fantasies soar,
Sleepy heads explore the lore.

Whispers of Friendship in the Dark

In shadows soft, we share our dreams,
Whispered secrets, gentle gleams.
With hearts aglow, fears take flight,
In the cozy arms of night.

Through silent tales, our spirits soar,
Bound by trust, we seek for more.
In the night's embrace, we find our place,
A friendship bright, a warm embrace.

Stitching Dreams with Laughter

With needle thread, our dreams we seam,
In laughter's glow, we weave a beam.
Each stitch a tale, each giggle bright,
Together we dance, in pure delight.

Through ups and downs, we gather round,
In every joy, our hearts are found.
With every tear, we sew anew,
Stitching our lives, just me and you.

Starlit Adventures in Pajamas

In pajamas soft, we roam the night,
Under starlit skies, dreams take flight.
With laughter loud, and hearts so free,
Adventure calls, just you and me.

Through fields of dreams, we spin and twirl,
Chasing moonbeams, in a magical whirl.
With whispered wishes, we touch the stars,
Creating memories, just ours, just ours.

Cocoa Wishes and Starry Nights

With mugs in hand, we share the warmth,
Cocoa wishes, stitched from charm.
Under starry skies, we dream and sip,
Of adventures grand, on a friendship trip.

In the cozy glow, all worries cease,
With every sip, we find our peace.
Together we drift, on night's sweet sigh,
Cocoa dreams dance, as the stars reply.

Sleepover Junction: Where Fun Meets Dreams.

In the glow of the twilight, laughter flows,
Friends gather round where the magic grows.
Games and giggles fill the night air,
A world of wonder, free from care.

Pillow fights burst like clouds above,
Whispers of secrets, the vibe is love.
With snacks and stories to share and spin,
At Sleepover Junction, the fun begins.

Midnight Whispers in Pajama Land

Stars peek through windows, twinkling bright,
In pajama land, we own the night.
With soft blankets wrapped around our feet,
Midnight whispers make the moment sweet.

Dreams take flight on our cozy beds,
Imagination soars, our hearts are led.
In the warmth of friendship, we feel so free,
In this magical realm, just you and me.

Dreamy Journeys on Soft Clouds

Climbing aboard on a fluffy cloud,
With open hearts, we dream out loud.
To lands of wonder, our minds set sail,
On this adventure, we cannot fail.

We dance with stars and chase the moon,
Each whispered promise, a sweet tune.
As dawn approaches, the journey slows,
But in our hearts, the magic glows.

Pillow Fort Adventures Await

In our pillow fort, a fortress high,
Imagination soars as we reach the sky.
With fairy lights twinkling, dreams take flight,
Together in this kingdom, everything's right.

Exploring the realms where wild tales lie,
In every corner, a new world to try.
With every giggle, the night is bright,
Pillow fort adventures, pure delight.

Reminiscence in Pillow Talk

Whispers linger in the night,
Softly shared with gentle light.
Memories dance on clouds of dreams,
In quiet corners, love redeems.

Moments wrapped in velvet sighs,
Where laughter fades, and truth replies.
Under stars, the past unfurls,
In the warmth of midnight pearls.

Each secret told, a heartbeat's trace,
Woven softly in this space.
Whispers echo through the dark,
As dreams ignite with every spark.

The night grows old, yet we remain,
In the comfort of our chain.
Together here, where shadows blend,
In pillow talk, we transcend.

The Fabric of Friendship and Dreams

Threads of laughter intertwine,
Stitched with hope, a grand design.
Each moment shared, a vibrant hue,
In the fabric, strong and true.

Through storms we stand, side by side,
In every tear, we find our pride.
Woven tales of joy and strife,
Crafting a tapestry of life.

Hand in hand, we chase the stars,
Mapping dreams with tiny scars.
In every fold, a story told,
Rich in warmth, never cold.

Together we weave the days ahead,
In the colors our hearts spread.
A patchwork quilt of love's embrace,
In friendship's arms, we find our place.

Fantasies on a Soft Canvas

Brush strokes whisper on the page,
Creating worlds, a vibrant stage.
Colors blend, and dreams ignite,
On a canvas stitched from light.

Gentle hues of twilight's glow,
A dance of visions, ebb and flow.
Each stroke a heartbeat, wild and free,
In this realm, we dare to be.

Imagination paints the skies,
With every glance, the spirit flies.
In this space, let shadows play,
As fantasies forever stay.

A masterpiece of dreams we write,
In colors bold, and whispers light.
On this soft canvas, we believe,
In every dream, we dare to weave.

Laughter on the Night Breeze

Whispers dance on gentle air,
Echoes of joy, light as fair.
Moonlit smiles are shared with ease,
Laughter carries on the breeze.

The stars above twinkle in glee,
Sharing secrets, just you and me.
Softly we sway, hearts entwined,
In this moment, pure bliss we find.

A fleeting joy, yet so profound,
In every giggle, love is found.
The night is ours, a sacred space,
Where laughter blooms, a warm embrace.

As shadows blend with evening's hue,
With every chuckle, our spirits renew.
In the quiet, silence speaks,
Laughter lingers, joy it seeks.

Stolen Moments Under the Stars

In the stillness, time stands still,
Stolen glances, hearts to fill.
Underneath the cosmic flow,
We find our way, let feelings grow.

Whispers soft like evening dew,
Secrets shared, just me and you.
The stars align in the night sky,
Each twinkle reflects our sighs.

A fleeting touch, electric spark,
In this moment, light ignites the dark.
The universe conspires with grace,
In stolen moments, we find our place.

Together here, with breath held tight,
In the wonder of a starry night.
These whispered dreams ignite our hearts,
As the cosmos plays its ageless parts.

Winks of Friendship in the Dark

In shadows deep, where silence falls,
Friendship winks, as laughter calls.
With just a glance, the world feels bright,
In the embrace of the velvety night.

A quiet nod, a knowing grin,
In these moments, our souls begin.
Through thick and thin, we share our plight,
Holding each other within the night.

The flicker of hope, a lantern's glow,
Guiding us through where the fears flow.
In darkness, we find strength and cheer,
With every wink, our hearts draw near.

Together we stand as twilight fades,
In this bond, our trust cascades.
Winks of friendship, strong and true,
In the unique glow, it's me and you.

Stories Weaving Through Soft Shadows

Under the cloak of quiet night,
Whispers weave, stories take flight.
In shadows soft, tales are spun,
Of laughter shared and battles won.

Each heartbeat paints a vibrant hue,
Colors of memories, old and new.
In the tapestry of time, we find,
A thread of love that's intertwined.

Softly spoke, the stories flow,
Through every glance and subtle glow.
In echoes past, our spirits soar,
Through whispered tales, we learn to explore.

So gather close, let shadows dance,
In stories woven, we find our chance.
Together, we'll craft a world so vast,
Where love and friendship forever last.

Nighttime Rides to Enchanted Places

Under a blanket of stars,
The moon guides our way,
Whispers of magic rise,
As dreams start to play.

Wheels turn on soft grass,
As fireflies dance near,
Every moment a spell,
In the dark, light appears.

Branches sway gently high,
In the cool evening air,
Stories unfold in night,
With secrets to share.

Time pauses its march,
In this twilight embrace,
Rides linger forever,
To enchanted places.

Tales from the Comfort Zone

Nestled in shadows warm,
With blankets piled high,
Stories come alive,
As the night draws nigh.

Coffee brews in the pot,
The clock ticks along,
Each page a journey,
In a world where we belong.

Laughter echoes softly,
Amid the gentle glow,
Every tale a treasure,
That only we know.

Time slips through our hands,
Yet we hold it more tight,
In this cozy embrace,
Everything feels right.

Cozy Connections on the Soft Rails

Winding through quiet towns,
On trains late at night,
Whispers of strangers blend,
In the lantern's light.

Warmth spreads through the car,
As stories intertwine,
Familiar yet strange,
These journeys are divine.

Hearts beat in rhythm,
With the soft rolling sound,
Each stop brings us closer,
New friendships abound.

In a world that is vast,
These moments feel home,
Cozy connections made,
As we traverse and roam.

Echoes of Laughter in a Sleepy Town

In the quiet of dusk,
Where shadows begin to play,
Laughter spills from porches,
As the sun fades away.

Children chase fireflies,
As the stars blink awake,
Joy dances in the air,
With each giggle they make.

Whispers of old bedtime tales,
Carried by the breeze,
Wrap the town in warmth,
Like comforting memories.

In this sleepy embrace,
The world feels just right,
Echoes of laughter shared,
In the calm of the night.

Whispers on the Wind

Softly secrets in the breeze,
Carried gently through the trees,
Moonlight dances on the ground,
In each whisper, peace is found.

Stars above begin to gleam,
Lifting spirits like a dream,
Nature's voice, a sweet caress,
In the night, we find our rest.

Leaves flutter, a gentle song,
In this place, we all belong,
Close your eyes, let worries fade,
In this hush, new hopes are made.

Echoes linger in the dark,
Kindred souls, we leave our mark,
Through the night, the whispers call,
Hear the magic, hear it all.

Slumber by the Station

Trains roll past with gentle sighs,
As the moonlight paints the skies,
Dreams take flight on midnight rails,
While the world around us pales.

Tickets tucked in pockets tight,
Whispers float into the night,
Crickets sing a lullaby,
As the stars begin to fly.

Sleepy eyes begin to close,
In the night, the stillness grows,
Here by the station's soft embrace,
Time itself begins to chase.

Rest your head upon the track,
Close your eyes, don't look back,
In the shadows, dreams are spun,
Slumber softly, morning's sun.

The Pajama Parade

Footed pjs on the street,
Little ones with laughter sweet,
Slipping down the neighborhood,
Happiness is understood.

Boys and girls in bright delight,
As the stars begin to light,
Under moonbeams, they will sway,
Join the joyful pajama parade.

Teddy bears tucked under arms,
Charming friends with tender charms,
With each step, the laughter grows,
In their hearts, the magic flows.

Through the night, the children roam,
Every street feels just like home,
Slumber waits, but here they play,
In the glow of their bright display.

Nighttime Adventures in Cozy Cars

Softly purring engines hum,
Underneath the stars, we come,
Windows down, let breezes in,
Feeling free, our hearts begin.

The moonlight guides our winding way,
In cozy cars, we laugh and play,
Adventures call, so off we steer,
Each mile brings more joy and cheer.

Stories shared beneath the sky,
As constellations loom up high,
Driving on through night's embrace,
The world transforms, we find our place.

With every turn, new sights to see,
The night unfolds its mystery,
In cozy cars, together we roam,
In this journey, we find our home.

The Great Pajama Expedition

In pajamas bright and bold,
We set off on quests untold.
With dreams as our guiding star,
We'll wander near and far.

Under the glow of the moonlight,
Imagination takes its flight.
Each corner hides a thrill,
Adventure waits, we feel the chill.

Exploring worlds of fluff and fun,
Chasing shadows, we all run.
In the kingdom of our sleep,
Treasures waiting, ours to keep.

As dawn approaches, time to rest,
In slumber, we find our best.
With dreams that sparkle and gleam,
The world will wait, it's just a dream.

Adventures Beyond the Pillow Fort

Behind the pillows, dreams arise,
A fortress built beneath the skies.
With courage, we face the night,
In this haven, hearts take flight.

Whispers of magic fill the air,
Creatures lurking, everywhere.
With laughter, we summon the brave,
In our fort, we learn to save.

A map of stars, we start to chart,
Every corner holds a part.
With friends beside, there's nothing wrong,
Against the world, we stand strong.

As dawn's light kisses our cheeks,
Adventure dreams, though they may peak,
We'll hold them tight, forevermore,
For every night brings a new lore.

Night Sky Journeys with Friends

Under the vast, twinkling sky,
With friends, we dream and fly.
Shooting stars whisper our name,
In the night, we play the game.

Galaxies spin, we choose our fate,
On cosmic ships, we navigate.
With laughter loud, we soar so high,
With every wish, we touch the sky.

Together we stitch the night with gleams,
Filling our heads with wild dreams.
Exploring each shimmer and light,
On this journey, hearts feel light.

As the morning beckons, we descend,
But in our hearts, the stars extend.
For every night, the magic stays,
In friendships true, we find our ways.

Mirthfulness Under the Blanket Fort

Tucked beneath our colorful sheets,
Laughter echoes, joy completes.
In our fort, we weave our tales,
With giggles floating like soft gales.

Pillows piled, our fortress strong,
In our haven, we all belong.
With stories shared and secrets told,
In the warmth, we chase the cold.

Beneath the blanket, shadows dance,
Every moment, a joyful chance.
Together we'll sing our favorite songs,
In our world, nothing feels wrong.

As the stars peek through the night,
We hold tight to this pure delight.
For when the world feels far apart,
We find our joy, we find our heart.

The Magical Night Express

Train of stars that softly gleam,
Chugging through a silver dream.
Whispers of the moonlight glow,
On a path where wishes flow.

Clocks strike twelve, the journey starts,
Carried through the world's fine arts.
Past the fields of sleepy dreams,
Where the night air gently seems.

Children laugh, their faces bright,
Riding on the magic light.
Hopping on this wondrous train,
Traveling through joy and pain.

Soon the dawn will come to play,
But for now, we'll softly sway.
In this magical night, we soar,
Dreams await behind each door.

Pajama Parade in Dreamland

In the land where night unfolds,
Pajama-clad, brave dreams we hold.
Marching in a soft parade,
Through the stars our joys are laid.

Balloons made of candy hues,
Guiding us through twilight views.
Dancing by the moonlight's grace,
Every child a smiling face.

Clouds are pillows, soft and wide,
On this merry, whimsical ride.
Skipping, laughing, all around,
In this dreamy, joyful sound.

As the night begins to fade,
Memories of our grand parade.
In our hearts, we'll keep the glow,
Of the fun we've come to know.

A Scenic Route Through Lullabies

On the gentle river's sweep,
Lullabies will help us sleep.
Melodies of breezes sigh,
Carried softly through the sky.

Each note dances with the stars,
Winding softly, near and far.
Taking dreams on cloud-like rides,
Where adventure gently hides.

Moonlit paths of silver streams,
Guide us through the land of dreams.
Kites of wishes fly above,
Sending whispers full of love.

As the night begins to care,
We find magic everywhere.
With each lullaby's embrace,
Dreams unfold in tender space.

Bedtime Bonanza at Dream Station

At the Dream Station, off we go,
To a place where soft winds blow.
Trains of dreams await our flight,
Beneath the twinkling, starry light.

Sleepyheads and cozy bears,
Gathered here without our cares.
Conductors made of stardust bright,
Guide us through the velvet night.

Hugs and laughter fill the air,
Magic slippers everywhere.
With our dreams, we make our way,
To adventures where we'll play.

As we ride on dreams so high,
Imaginations touch the sky.
At the Dream Station, we'll depart,
With sleepy smiles and happy hearts.

Midnight Whisper Train

In the quiet night, whispers flow,
The moonlight dances, soft and slow.
Stars twinkle high, a guiding light,
On the midnight train, dreams take flight.

The tracks gleam bright, a silver line,
Through valleys deep, the shadows twine.
Each gentle chug, a calming sound,
In slumber's arms, peace is found.

Windows open wide, breezes tease,
Wrapped in warmth, like autumn leaves.
The world outside begins to fade,
As hearts align in this magic made.

So ride with me, to dreams we steer,
With every pulse, there's joy sincere.
On the midnight whisper train, we glide,
Embracing wonders, side by side.

Pajama Dreams on Rails

Cotton clouds parade in hues,
Wearing stripes of pink and blues.
A train puffs past in sleepy grace,
Pajama dreams, a cozy space.

Moonbeams shine on drowsy heads,
As stories weave in snuggly beds.
Through sleepy towns, the engine hums,
While pillow forts become the drums.

Hush now, little one, don't you cry,
The starry nights will never lie.
The train of dreams is on its way,
In pajama glow, we'll drift and play.

With each soft breath, let worries cease,
In gentle rhythms, find your peace.
Pajama dreams on rails we ride,
Through starlit skies, forever wide.

Conductor of Giggles

In the heart of night, with a gentle grin,
The conductor smiles, where dreams begin.
With a wave of hands, laughter takes flight,
Giggles abound in the shimmering light.

Whistles blow and the train rolls on,
Chugging away 'til the break of dawn.
Every giggle's a starry boon,
Guiding us through with a silver tune.

From car to car, the joy flows free,
With playful hearts, it's jubilee.
The conductor's call, a laugh so sweet,
On this magical ride, hearts skip a beat.

So hold on tight, let the fun commence,
In giggles and joy, we find our sense.
With the conductor of giggles at the helm,
We'll journey through joy, in our dream-filled realm.

Choo-Choo Cuddles

On this train of cuddles, here we sway,
With every chug, we drift away.
Soft as whispers, warm as the sun,
Choo-choo cuddles, two become one.

Fluffy blankets wrapped so tight,
In a world of dreams, we take flight.
The gentle sway, a lullaby,
As stars peek in from the velvet sky.

Close your eyes, hear the sound,
Of soft chugs echoing all around.
With every giggle and gentle sigh,
Choo-choo cuddles, oh my, oh my!

The journey's sweet, let time unfold,
In our cozy train, warmth to behold.
Through wonders vast, our hearts we'll tease,
Choo-choo cuddles, pure love's breeze.

Giggles in the Twilight

Whispers of laughter ride the breeze,
Children at play among the trees.
Shadows dance as twilight falls,
Joyful echoes in the night calls.

Flickering fireflies twinkle bright,
Guiding the way, a magical sight.
Beneath the sky, soft and vast,
Innocent times, forever will last.

Silly stories we spin with glee,
Chasing dreams as wild as can be.
Under the stars, we find our peace,
In these moments, our hearts release.

As the night wraps us in its embrace,
With giggles lingering, we find our place.
The world fades away, just us, delight,
Forever in love with this twilight night.

Stars Beneath Our Sleeping Bags

Cocooned in warmth, our secrets shared,
With the universe, we are bared.
Ink-black skies adorned with light,
Stars twinkle softly, a wondrous sight.

Under the fabric, dreams take flight,
Imagination soars through the night.
We whisper tales of hero's quests,
As sleep steals softly, we lay our heads.

Each star a wish, a hope we hold,
In every glimmer, stories unfold.
Together we drift through the cosmic sea,
In this moment, just you and me.

With eyes closed tight, we slip away,
Into the magic of night and play.
Where dreams and starlight gently blend,
Beneath our bags, the night won't end.

Late-Night Secrets and Stardust

Under the moon's soft, silver glow,
We share secrets only we know.
Soft whispers carried on the breeze,
Wrapped in laughter, hearts at ease.

Stardust clings to our every word,
In the stillness, we've often heard.
Thoughts like fireflies dance and dart,
Bringing forth dreams, a new start.

Moonlit shadows weave between us,
Casting a spell, wild yet generous.
In the quiet, our spirits soar,
Late-night wonders, forevermore.

As the cosmos spins above our heads,
We'll hold these moments, where friendship spreads.
In twilight's embrace, we'll take our flight,
With secrets shared until the dawn's light.

Campfire Tales in Moonlight

Flickering flames dance in the dark,
A circle of friends, we've found our spark.
With gentle stories, we weave the night,
Campfire tales under the moonlight.

Shadows twist as the embers glow,
Mysterious legends from long ago.
Each whispered word, a spell we cast,
In this moment, the die is cast.

Laughter echoes into the trees,
As the night air carries our dreams with ease.
We share our fears, our hopes, our plans,
Bound together by invisible strands.

As the fire fades and we start to yawn,
We'll tuck these memories, as a new dawn.
In every tale, a part of our soul,
Our campfire tales forever make us whole.

Twilight Tales and Pillow Fights

Under soft blankets, we softly giggle,
Stories unfold, our worries dribble.
Shadows dance on the walls' embrace,
In this safe space, we find our place.

Pillows fly as laughter ignites,
Dancing giggles take on new heights.
Stars peek in through the window's light,
Filling dreams with magic tonight.

Secrets whispered, eyes full of dreams,
Charting our course on moonlit beams.
Adventures await in the land of sleep,
Where friendship's bond runs wide and deep.

With twilight tales, our hearts ignite,
In the glow of friendship, all feels right.
Together we weave our stories bright,
In the joy of these enchanted nights.

Sleepover Journeys

Outside, the night lays a peaceful shroud,
Inside, we talk, laughter fills the crowd.
With soda and snacks, our spirits rise,
Each little secret a sweet surprise.

We share our dreams, the hopes we hold,
In whispered tones, our lives unfold.
Blanket forts become castles grand,
Adventure awaits, so close at hand.

Every giggle is a wish in flight,
Together we soar into the night.
In the twilight glow, our fears take flight,
Guardians of dreams until morning light.

Sleepover journeys, a cherished ride,
With laughter as our constant guide.
In the world we build, there's no goodbye,
As stars above twinkle in the sky.

Midnight Snack Adventures

Underneath stars that brightly gleam,
Kitchen raids become our secret dream.
Cookies and milk, a delightful pair,
In our midnight quest, flavors we share.

Whispers spark with a thrill in the air,
Every nibble hides a tasty dare.
Chocolate sprinkles and chips abound,
In the still of night, joy can be found.

Laughter echoes as we munch away,
Making the most of our sleepover stay.
Each bite a treasure, each moment bright,
In this midnight kitchen, all feels right.

With crumbs on our faces and smiles wide,
Adventures unfold as we sit side by side.
In every crunch, our spirits soar,
Midnight snack adventures leave us wanting more.

Trackside Secrets and Silhouettes

By the tracks where the trains rush by,
We find our stories under the sky.
Whispers of dreams float in the night,
As silhouettes dance in the fading light.

Secrets hidden in the shadows deep,
Moments we treasure and vows we keep.
The train's rhythmic song, a soothing hum,
In this safe haven, we feel so numb.

With every shadow, a tale unfolds,
Of friendship forged and futures bold.
Underneath stars, our hearts take flight,
In trackside secrets, we find our light.

With laughter shared and dreams in sight,
Together we shine, our spirits bright.
As the trains thunder by, we hold tight,
In the magic of night, all feels right.

Silhouettes of Friendship

In the soft glow of the setting sun,
We reflect on the times, each cherished one.
With silhouettes cast upon the floor,
Each moment shared leaves us wanting more.

From whispered secrets to heartfelt laughs,
In the tapestry of life, we draw our paths.
With hands entwined, we face the fight,
In every shadow, our dreams ignite.

Old memories linger, like stars that shine,
Bonded by laughter, your heart in mine.
As day turns to night, our dreams take flight,
In the glow of friendship, everything feels right.

Silhouettes dancing, a beautiful sight,
Together we forge through every plight.
With love as our guide, we'll always stand,
In each other's hearts, hand in hand.

Pajama Picnic on the Train

In soft pajamas, we gather near,
A picnic spread on the comfy seats.
With giggles blending with the train's cheer,
We share our snacks and tasty treats.

The rhythmic clatter beneath the floor,
As we chat and laugh on our little ride.
Outside the window, landscapes pour,
A moving canvas, bright and wide.

With pillows tossed and blankets spread,
We sip our juice, and stories flow.
In every bite, our joy is fed,
Creating memories as we go.

The whistle blows, the journey sways,
Under the stars, we sigh and dream.
In pajama comfort, the night conveys,
A blissful peace like a flowing stream.

Lullabies along the Tracks

Whispers of dreams paint the night,
As train wheels hum a gentle tune.
Stars above begin to shine bright,
Lulling us under the watchful moon.

Soft voices sing of distant lands,
Carrying hopes on the soothing breeze.
Wrapped in warmth, we hold each hand,
Embracing the magic, hearts at ease.

With each mile, the worries fade,
Like shadows lost in fading light.
In this moment, a serenade,
We drift in dreams, till morning bright.

Lullabies fill the cozy space,
As night trains whisper their sweet refrain.
Through window frames, we see their grace,
In softest comfort, we remain.

Hugs and Heartbeats

In a little cabin, snug and warm,
Heartbeat echoes mingle with soft sighs.
Wrapped in blankets, safe from harm,
Each hug we share, the love just flies.

With every turn and gentle sway,
The train rocks softly, like a lullaby.
In twilight glow, we find our way,
As happiness blooms in every eye.

Laughter dances like light on the walls,
While memories shimmer like stars aglow.
In this space, where no one falls,
Hugs bind us close, in warmth they flow.

Every moment, a treasure we keep,
As journeys meld with the bond we form.
In this haven, promises seep,
Wrapped in love, we weather the storm.

Quirky Carriages of Comfort

Each carriage tells its own sweet tale,
With colors bright, a playful sight.
The seats adorned, where laughter prevails,
Creating joy from day to night.

Beneath the whims of overhead lights,
Passengers meet in whimsical glee.
Sharing secrets and silly flights,
In this patchwork of harmony.

A quirky seat with toys galore,
Imaginations soar in every heart.
In these carriages, the memories store,
Where laughter and dreams love to start.

Through windows, landscapes race away,
As stories blossom in the breeze.
In this train, we cherish the play,
Crafting a world where joy is free.

Tracks of Dreams Through Slumber

In the quiet night, whispers flow,
Footprints linger, soft and slow.
Through a field of stars we roam,
Creating worlds to call our own.

Each shadow hides a tale untold,
Mysteries in dreams unfold.
In slumber's arms, we take our flight,
Chasing visions through the night.

The echoes of the day now fade,
In moonlit paths, our fears allayed.
With every step, a heartbeat chimes,
Carving memories through space and time.

As dawn approaches, dreams take wing,
A fleeting touch, but what they bring.
In waking hours we'll glimpse the seam,
Of our woven tracks of dream.

Midnight Escapades on Pillowy Paths

Beneath the stars, we find our way,
On fluffy clouds, we laugh and play.
With every leap, we dance, we glide,
In midnight's embrace, we do not hide.

Whispers of night lead us astray,
In silken realms, we dream and sway.
Chasing fireflies, bright and bold,
Creating stories yet untold.

A gentle breeze sings lullabies,
As starlit secrets fill the skies.
We twirl on paths where wishes gleam,
In silver moments, lose the theme.

With each heartbeat, our spirits soar,
In the magic of night, forevermore.
A tapestry of dreams we weave,
In midnight escapades, we believe.

Serenity on the Horizon of Sleep

In the twilight's gentle sigh,
Serenity calls, inviting the shy.
The horizon glows, a velvet hue,
Where dreams awaken, fresh and new.

Crickets sing their nightly tune,
While stars embrace the silver moon.
With every breath, troubles cease,
Finding solace in the gentle peace.

The whispering winds weave through trees,
Carrying thoughts, like drifting leaves.
On the edge of slumber's grace,
We find our tranquil, sacred space.

As eyes grow heavy, spirits rise,
Floating softly towards the skies.
In this haven, we'll take our leap,
Into serenity, the heart of sleep.

Moonbeams and Magical Stories

Under moonbeams, tales unfold,
Of heroic hearts and treasures bold.
Each shimmering light a guiding spark,
Illuminating paths through the dark.

With every whisper, a story stays,
Adventures wrapped in starlit rays.
We sail on ships made of dreams,
Navigating life through magical themes.

The castle walls hold secrets tight,
Guarding wishes in the night.
Every glance, a spell, a vow,
In the realm of magic, here and now.

As dawn approaches, dreams collide,
Yet in our hearts, they still abide.
For every moonbeam holds the key,
To stories spun in mystery.

Friendship Dreams on a Silver Track

On a silver track, we glide with grace,
In dreams of laughter, we find our place.
Side by side, with hearts so bright,
Friendship blooms in the softest light.

Through winding paths, our spirits soar,
Holding hands, we long for more.
In whispered secrets, we weave our tales,
Together we conquer, where love prevails.

Stars above us, shining clear,
In every moment, we draw near.
With every heartbeat, our bond grows strong,
In the symphony of life, it's where we belong.

As twilight fades, and dawn breaks free,
In the world of dreams, just you and me.
Together we journey, hand in hand,
On the silver track, forever we'll stand.

Twilight Treasures at the Pillow Junction

Pillows soft, where dreams collide,
In twilight's glow, our hopes abide.
Whispers flutter like the evening breeze,
Treasures found with such sweet ease.

As stars awake, we share our lore,
In the quiet night, we dare explore.
Secrets hidden beneath the moon,
At pillow junction, we sing our tune.

Soft laughter dances in the air,
Creating moments, beyond compare.
With every glance, our spirits lift,
In the twilight treasures, love is the gift.

Sleepy eyes and wishes made,
In the gentle night, our worries fade.
Together we dream, our futures bright,
At pillow junction, heart's delight.

Sleepy Hugs and Moonlit Views

Under the stars, we find our rest,
Sleepy hugs are truly the best.
With moonlit views, the world feels right,
In your embrace, I drift each night.

Gentle whispers, sweet and low,
In the quiet night, our feelings grow.
With every heartbeat, dreams take flight,
Together, we shine, a beacon of light.

Magic lingers in the midnight air,
Wrapped in warmth, we shed our cares.
In slumber's arms, we're safe and sound,
In sleepy hugs, love's bliss is found.

As dawn awakes, we'll greet the day,
With golden rays, they'll guide our way.
Through every moment, we will imbue,
The warmth of sleep and moonlit views.

Chasing Clouds with Laughter

Up in the sky, where the clouds abound,
Chasing dreams, laughter is found.
With every giggle, our spirits arise,
In the game of life, we're the blue skies.

Running through fields, with joy in our gaze,
In carefree moments, we dance and blaze.
Together we wander, hand in hand,
Chasing clouds in a whimsical land.

With every breeze, we feel so alive,
In the heart of laughter, we learn to thrive.
Through sunshine and rain, our joy unfurls,
In the tapestry of life, we paint our worlds.

So let us soar, higher and free,
In the chase of clouds, just you and me.
With laughter as our guiding song,
In this joyful journey, we both belong.

Driftwood and Dreamlines

On shores of silver sand, they lay,
Driftwood whispers tales of the bay.
Dreamlines twist in the evening air,
Guiding souls to places rare.

Stars wink softly, a night's embrace,
Echoes of laughter in time and space.
Each wooden form, a story told,
Of seas once crossed, and dreams so bold.

Tide pulls gently, a rhythmic dance,
As moonlight weaves a mystic trance.
Forgotten wishes on branches cling,
In the heart of night, the dreamlines sing.

Resting dreams on a sandy bed,
While the waves hum softly, lightly spread.
Driftwood waits for the break of dawn,
Where memories fade but hope lives on.

Twilight Tracks and Teddies

In twilight's glow, soft shadows play,
Tracks of the day slowly drift away.
Teddies sit by the fire's warm light,
Whispering secrets, a hush of night.

Stars emerge, twinkling bright and clear,
While comforting tales melt away fear.
Adventures await in every dream,
As moonbeams dance by the night's gentle stream.

With little paws and button eyes bright,
Teddies guard hearts till dawn's first light.
Twilight tracks that the shadows cast,
Lead us gently through memories vast.

Wrapped in warmth, we chart the skies,
With dreams of adventures and whispered sighs.
In twilight, magic weaves its thread,
Holding us close till we're safely fed.

Whimsical Whistles and Wishes

In gardens where the wildflowers sway,
Whimsical whistles call us to play.
Wishes take flight on the back of the breeze,
Dancing with laughter among the trees.

Pinwheels spin, colors burst bright,
Each turn a wish floating into the night.
Giggles and whispers weave through the air,
Making moments so precious and rare.

Beneath the stars, dreams start to bloom,
As echoes of laughter fill every room.
Whistling winds carry tales untold,
Of hopes and journeys, of hearts bold.

In the charm of the moon's gentle glow,
We hold our wishes, we let them flow.
Whimsical rhythms guide us along,
In a dance of delight, we forever belong.

Cozy Cabin Chronicles

In a cabin warm, where the fire glows,
Chronicles wrapped in velvety prose.
With window views of the snow-kissed pines,
Life slows down, where the heart aligns.

Laughter rings through the wooden beams,
Sipping cocoa, lost in dreams.
Stories shared by the crackling flame,
Each moment cherished, never the same.

Outside, the world is a blanket of white,
While in our haven, all feels right.
Footprints fade on the frosted ground,
As love and warmth in the cabin resound.

With blankets piled and hearts aglow,
We write our tales with a steady flow.
Cozy cabin, a shelter divine,
In your embrace, our dreams entwine.

Sleepy Eyes and Smiling Hearts

In the quiet of the night,
Dreams begin to take their flight.
Soft whispers on the breeze,
Bringing calm and gentle ease.

Pillow fights of laughter loud,
Wrapped in warmth, love is proud.
Sleepy eyes and hearts that glow,
In this moment, joy will flow.

Stars are twinkling up above,
Wrapping all in tender love.
Every giggle, every sigh,
Carries hope that will not die.

As dawn creeps in, we'll awake,
With fond memories to make.
Together, we'll greet the day,
In our hearts, forever stay.

The Journey of Warmth and Laughter

On a winding path we tread,
With laughter as our thread.
Every step a joyful song,
For in love, we all belong.

Sunlit days and starlit nights,
Share our dreams and take our flights.
Filling spaces with our cheer,
In this journey, you are near.

Mountains high and rivers wide,
With you, I feel so much pride.
Through the storms and in the sun,
Together, we are always one.

Fireside chats and stories told,
In each moment, treasures unfold.
The warmth we share, like a spark,
It guides us through the endless dark.

Evening Adventures in Cozy Corners

In corners where shadows play,
Evening whispers a soft lay.
Candles flicker, shadows dance,
We find magic in a glance.

Hot cocoa warms both hands and heart,
From this spot, we won't depart.
With every sip, we find our way,
In cozy corners, we will stay.

The world outside begins to fade,
In our haven, love's displayed.
Each cherished laugh, each gentle jest,
Within these walls, we feel our best.

As night deepens, we ignite,
The spark of dreams that feels so right.
With whispered hopes and soft goodnight,
In our realm, all is bright.

Playful Spirits under Moonlit Skies

Underneath the silver glow,
Starlit paths where dreamers go.
Laughter dances on the breeze,
As we wander 'neath the trees.

With playful hearts, we chase the night,
Every moment feels so right.
Jumping shadows, joyful cries,
Playful spirits under skies.

Moonlight casts a magic spell,
In this realm, all is well.
Every secret shared with glee,
Building bonds, just you and me.

Through the whispers of the dark,
We will find our inner spark.
In this dance, we will remain,
Bound together, free from pain.

Sweet Dreams on the Horizon

In the twilight, whispers play,
Softly guiding dreams away.
Stars unlock their glowing light,
Chasing shadows into night.

Clouds of silver drift and glide,
As the day begins to hide.
Hopes like fireflies gently gleam,
Awake within our sweetest dream.

Moonbeams dance on pillows low,
While the world begins to slow.
With each breath, the night unfolds,
Stories waiting to be told.

Close your eyes and take the flight,
Into realms of pure delight.
Sweet dreams rise on evening's breeze,
Carried softly through the trees.

The Train of Cozy Companions

All aboard the friendly train,
Chugging softly through the rain.
Pillows piled, laughter rings,
Cozy warmth that comfort brings.

Friends together, side by side,
Through the night, we will ride.
Stories shared, secrets told,
In this warmth, we feel so bold.

Outside, the world is a blur,
Inside, laughter starts to stir.
With a mug of cocoa near,
All our worries disappear.

Rolling on, with hearts aglow,
Past the stars, we gently go.
Each moment sweet, each hug a boon,
Riding along 'neath the smiling moon.

Blankets and Giggles Unraveled

Underneath a warm cocoon,
Giggles rise like a happy tune.
Blankets piled, a fortress made,
In this space, no fears invade.

Fluffy clouds and twilight's song,
In this haven, we belong.
With each laugh, the night feels bright,
In our world of sweet delight.

Tickle fights and whispered dreams,
Laughter flows like silver streams.
With every joy and silly game,
We are free to be the same.

Softly snuggled in our nest,
Feeling safe, we are so blessed.
As the stars hang overhead,
We embrace the dreams we tread.

Nighttime Adventures on Cotton Tracks

Under stars, our dreams take flight,
On cotton tracks wrapped in night.
With each step, the shadows play,
Leading us on our magical way.

Glowing lanterns, spirits rise,
As we journey through the skies.
Chasing whispers, feeling free,
Adventures call, just you and me.

Through the fields of twinkling lights,
Hand in hand, we share our sights.
Every heartbeat, every laugh,
Guides us forward on our path.

Nighttime's secrets, gently shared,
In this moment, we are dared.
With the moon as our delight,
Together we embrace the night.

The Carousel of Cozy Nights

The stars twinkle softly above,
As shadows dance with gentle light.
Wrapped in warmth, we share our love,
In the carousel of cozy nights.

A blanket fort, our secret space,
With whispered dreams drifting near.
Laughter and joy find their place,
In the heart of night, we shed our fear.

The moon reflects our playful glee,
As we spin in circles, hand in hand.
Time stands still, wild and free,
In this magical, enchanted land.

So close your eyes and hold on tight,
As we twirl beneath the glowing sky.
In this realm of dreams, pure delight,
Together, we laugh and softly sigh.

Slippers and Silhouette Dreams

With slippers on, we roam the night,
Through shadows cast by flickering light.
Silhouette dreams begin to play,
In the corners where whispers stay.

The clock ticks slow, time melts away,
As we wander in our own ballet.
Each step a story, softly spun,
In the magic of the day, we've won.

Candle flames flicker, shadows sway,
Enchanted moments lead the way.
With every sigh and every stare,
We breathe in dreams that fill the air.

As morning breaks with golden beams,
We hold onto our silhouette dreams.
With slippers on, our hearts take flight,
We dance together into the light.

Chasing Nighttime Explorations

Underneath the vibrant stars,
We chase the whispers of the night.
Adventures beckon from afar,
Through moonlit paths, our dreams take flight.

With every step, a secret glows,
A twinkling promise, bold and bright.
Across the fields where the wild grass grows,
We wander deeper in the quiet night.

The echo of laughter fills the air,
As shadows guide us on our way.
In this journey, we shed our care,
Lost in explorations, we'll stay.

With hearts aglow and spirits high,
We chase the tales that stars bestow.
In every moonbeam, every sigh,
We find the magic that helps us grow.

A Train Ride Through Dreamy Realms

All aboard the train of dreams,
With windows wide to the starlit skies.
We journey forth on silver beams,
As twilight deepens, magic flies.

The whistle blows, the cars sway mild,
Through valleys deep and mountains tall.
Like a curious, wandering child,
We capture wonders, one and all.

Each stop unveils a story true,
Of lands where dreams and fantasies meet.
Through forests lush and oceans blue,
Adventure calls, we feel the beat.

As dawn approaches, gently glows,
The train rolls on, our spirits soar.
In this realm, only love knows,
The beauty found in every door.

Moonlit Memories on Wheels

Under a pale, whispering moon,
The wheels of time softly croon.
Stars twinkle like secrets told,
Memories of journeys bold.

Taking the road less traveled bright,
Guided by dreams in the night.
Each mile a story we weave,
In the magic that we believe.

With laughter echoing far and wide,
Our hearts a compass, our dreams our guide.
Moonlit paths where shadows play,
In the realm where wishes stay.

Together we dance through the breeze,
With whispered hopes that bring us ease.
Wheels spinning tales both old and new,
In this moonlit ride, just me and you.

Sleepytime Whistle Stop

The whistle blows, a lullaby,
As evening clouds drift by.
Drowsy tunes fill the air,
At this quiet, sleepy lair.

Trains of dreams come rolling in,
Softly calling us to begin.
Gentle rhythms of peace abound,
In the stillness, love is found.

Hopes wrapped in blankets snug,
In this cozy little hug.
Time pauses, moments hang,
At this stop, sweet memories sang.

So close your eyes, let dreams arise,
Under the velvet, starry skies.
Hold on tight, let the journey start,
At sleepytime, we warm the heart.

Journeying through Dreamscapes

Floating on clouds of shimmering dreams,
Where nothing is quite as it seems.
Colorful echoes of laughter ring,
In this world where our wishes take wing.

Mountains of candy, rivers of light,
Chasing the moon through the velvet night.
Each step a dance, each glance a thrill,
In this magical land, time stands still.

Whispers of wishes in the breeze,
Carried gently among the trees.
Adventure awaits just ahead,
In the tapestry of dreams, we're led.

With every heartbeat, the scenes unfold,
Throughout the night, our stories told.
Journeying onward, hand in hand,
Together forever in dreamland's strand.

Conductor of Nighttime Nonsense

With a cap on my head, I take my place,
As the stars wink bright in this wondrous space.
I wave my lantern to gather the crew,
For a ride on the tracks of whimsy and dew.

The train whistles softly, a jolly old sound,
As we venture through landscapes where laughter is found.
Puppies in top hats and cats with a flair,
Join in the fun as we wander without care.

Each station we stop, a new tale unfolds,
With pirates, and fairies, and treasures of gold.
The night dances on, a whimsical blend,
As the conductor of nonsense, I lead to the end.

So hold tight your dreams, take a ride on this train,
Through laughter and joy, we'll dance in the rain.
In the realm of the silly, the sweet, and the bright,
Together we'll play through the magical night.

Slumbering Across Cozy Fields

In the hush of twilight's glow,
Soft blankets wrap us, hearts aglow.
Moonlit whispers fill the air,
Dreams take flight without a care.

Gentle breezes kiss our skin,
Lullabies of evening spin.
Stars above begin to gleam,
Guiding us through every dream.

Fields of night with shadows play,
As we drift, the world fades away.
Crickets sing their nightly tune,
As we sway beneath the moon.

Time pauses in this sacred place,
Slumber's hold, a warm embrace.
In the quiet, we find peace,
In our dreams, our joys increase.

Sleepover Serenades Under the Stars

Giggles echo, secrets shared,
Underneath the night, we dared.
Blankets spread on lawn so wide,
With a friend right by your side.

Stories told by firelight's spark,
Imagination free to embark.
Dreams unfurl like wings in flight,
In the magic of the night.

Stars above begin to hum,
Softly whispering, 'Here we come.'
Pillowed heads in joyful glee,
In this moment, we are free.

Sleepover magic wraps us tight,
Cares dissolve in sheer delight.
Together in this dance we find,
The bonds of friendship intertwined.

The Voyage of Whispering Friends

Sailing on a sea of dreams,
Whispers float like silken beams.
With the tide, our spirits rise,
Underneath the endless skies.

Charting paths through realms unknown,
Together on this journey grown.
Hearts and laughter fill the air,
In this voyage, love laid bare.

Through stormy skies and sunny rays,
Friendship guides us through the maze.
Hand in hand, we face the night,
In our hearts, a spark of light.

As we sail on waves of trust,
In each other, we find the gust.
Whispers echo, dreams ignite,
Forever bound, our souls take flight.

Pajama Quest in the Dreamscape

In our pajamas soft and warm,
We embark on dreams that charm.
With sleepy eyes, we venture far,
Chasing stardust, near and far.

Through the clouds that swirl and weave,
In this realm, we dare believe.
Fairy tales and wishes blend,
On this quest, our hearts transcend.

Magic paths of shimmering light,
Lead us through the velvet night.
With laughter ringing, we explore,
Every dream a new door.

Together we will dance and glide,
In this dreamscape, side by side.
Pajama clad, we take our flight,
In the realms where dreams unite.

Tracks of Laughter

In fields where children play, their giggles soar,
Joy on the breeze, a never-ending roar.
Footsteps of happiness dance on the ground,
Echoes of laughter, a sweet, joyous sound.

Beneath the warm sun, we skip and we run,
Chasing the moments, pure bliss just begun.
With pockets of sunshine, our spirits are high,
Painting the canvas where memories lie.

In the evening glow, stories take flight,
Whispers of laughter echo through the night.
Around the warm fire, we share tales anew,
Where tracks of laughter weave dreams that come true.

The stars sparkle bright, as we bid day adieu,
With hearts full of joy, the horizon feels true.
Together forever, on this joyous track,
We'll cherish the laughter and always look back.

Slumber Odyssey

In the hush of the night, where dreams gently glide,
A slumbering voyage begins to decide.
Soft pillows of clouds, in a shadowy sea,
We drift through the whispers, where wishes roam free.

Moonbeams like lanterns, guiding the way,
Through valleys of stars, where the wild creatures play.
In realms filled with magic, adventures unfold,
With stories of valor that never grow old.

A kingdom of slumber, where all fears dissolve,
As dreams spin their tales, our hopes they involve.
From the depths of the night, new journeys arise,
On this odyssey of sleep, we learn how to fly.

As dawn softly breaks, we awaken with grace,
The treasures we found are ours to embrace.
In the light of the day, we carry the spark,
Of our slumbering journeys, igniting the dark.

Dreamland Expressway

A highway of dreams, where the visions collide,
We journey through wonder on this timeless ride.
With headlights of starlight illuminating the path,
We speed through the night, with laughter and wrath.

Each mile holds a secret, a tale to unfold,
Landscapes of memories, both treasured and bold.
Through valleys of twilight, and hills made of night,
We dance with the shadows till morning's first light.

In the rearview, the worries of day,
Dissolve in the mist, like the fog far away.
Side by side, we capture the essence of fun,
On the dreamland expressway, our spirits can run.

As dawn's rosy fingers stretch across the sky,
We park at the station, as dreams whisper goodbye.
But the journey continues, in hearts, it will stay,
On this dreamland expressway, we'll always find play.

Starlit Pillow Forts

In the glow of the moon, where dreams come alive,
Starlit pillow forts help our imaginations thrive.
Blanket castles towering, sturdy and bright,
A refuge of wonder, our own world of light.

With whispered adventures, each corner a tale,
Guarded by shadows, our giggles set sail.
Through galaxies woven from laughter and cheer,
We journey as heroes, untouched by our fear.

As the night softly wanes, we huddle in close,
Wrapped in the warmth, a comforting dose.
The stars keep their watch, as we dream and explore,
In our starlit pillow forts, we're forever more.

And when dawn begins to unfurl the day's light,
We'll treasure our fort, and the dreams of the night.
For in every night's magic, we find our true place,
In starlit pillow forts, where dreams interlace.